SONG OF THE LAST SHAMAN

(A SANE AIR)

WORDS AND MUSIC: AL SENERCHIA

PHOTOGRAPHIC LIGHTWORK: RICHARD DUFFY

DUFF PRINTING & PUBLISHING CO.
R.R. 2 BOX 1048
HONESDALE, PA 18431

Duff Printing & Publishing Company
RR 2 Box 1048 Honesdale, Pennsylvania 18431

International Standard Book Number 0-9637076-0-4
Library of Congress Catalog Number 93-71628

An Acknowledgement

"The purpose of connecting (Being Centered) is Perpetuality."

That statement, along with its Meaning felt, was conveyed to me early this year by a Brother whom some of us call Rajpur. Many people refer to Him and His "Brothers and Sisters" as Ascended Masters, Guardian Angels, Guides and so on. What is most Real in the experience of connecting with Them is the feeling — a feeling of Indivisibility: the Meaning of Peace.

Our willingness to *connect with our Peace* is the Movement of Creation acknowledged, our Divinity recognized.

As we trust into Soul — the experience of Being — we release the private sense of control that interprets and defines.

When Richard Duffy and I first met to explore the possibility of the book you now have in hand, an interesting connection was shared. An hour before our meeting I was delighted to read that the word "Rhine" (like the European river) found its source in the word "flow." *Staying with the flow* I experienced an expansion of that initial delight — an expansion that seemed to promise fulfillment, the nature of which would surely reveal the Truth that all words, indeed all things had their source in That Flow . . . the book I was reading did not go that far, but I did feel very good about Everything. The exquisitely natural unreasonableness of that good feeling sang thru my Being accompanied by the words "The Unity Of Infinity constitutes Absolute Simplicity," as I shoveled the ashes out of the living room fireplace. A new fire was about to be lighted.

Richard arrived and placed into my hands the lighting match: the Rinehart photographs. The Heart Flow we felt was undeniable. The Heart Flow Is undeniable.

Encouraging all of us to allow ourselves to be what we already Are in Actuality, our Friend Raj says about Love: "If you have let a little bit thru, you have let all of what it Means thru."

Aloha,
Al Senerchia
April 18, 1993 K

THE REMEMBER RING
AND THE GATHER RING
ARE THE SOUNDNESS
OF CONSCIOUSING.
SING.

THIS IS FOR YOU. . .

Infinity Is in the Air. . .

THE FIRST BOW WAS A MUSICAL INSTRUMENT.

URFA, THE FIRST SHAMAN, "HEARD HIS LIGHT."

Divine Order Is Harmony.

© 1898
F.A. RINEHART
OMAHA

HARMONY IS PEACE.

THE SIMPLICITY OF INFINITE BEING IS THE MOVEMENT OF CREATION WITHIN EACH AND EVERY ONE OF US.

Honoring Equality dissolves all equations, reveals Completeness, Oneness.

©F.A. RINEHART
OMAHA

THE HEART CAN NOT FLOW TRULY
WHEN THE HAND IS A FIST.

©F.A. RINEHART
OMAHA

THE ONLY DEAL IS TO HEAL.
TO HEAL IS THE ONLY DEAL.
YIELD.

©1800
F.A. RINEHART
OMAHA

Unity Is You
experiencing Your Divine Birthright.

© 1898
F.A. RINEHART
OMAHA

RHYTHM RHYMES,

FLOWERS FLOW,

PEACE IS. . .

INFLUX, PENETRATION, REVELATION

© 1898
F.A. RINEHART
OMAHA

AS SMOKE SIGNALS FROM ONE PLACE
TO ANOTHER EXPRESS COMMUNICATION,
COMMUNION IS BEING WITH
THE DIRECT SOURCE OF LIGHT.

THE WIND CAN NOT BLOW AWAY
THAT WHICH IS STILL WITHIN ITSELF —
THAT WHICH IS ITSELF THE WIND,
AT HOME.

OUR PATHS THRU A DESERT OF DIVISION
EVAPORATE IN THE SWEET AIR OF ONENESS
UNFOLDING.
THE INEVITABLE BLOSSOMS OF HERE AND NOW
EXPRESS THAT AWARENESS, THAT SPIRIT.

THE WILLINGNESS TO EMBRACE
THE DIVINE ESSENCE OF YOUR SELF
IS LETTING INFINITY BE
WHAT IT IS BEING.
THIS IS FULL CIRCLE.

FROM YOUR CENTER
COMMUNICATION REVEALS
THE ULTIMATE PURPOSE:
COMMUNION WITH ALL.
LOVE, INTEGRITY, UNITY.

FEATHERS FREE
ANCHOR LIGHT,
BALANCE SINGS

LEVELING CENTURIES OF DOUBT
LEVELING MOUNTAINS OF MISTRUST

THE ONLY WORK THAT IS LEFT
(AND RIGHT)
IS TO BESTOW UPON YOURSELF
THE GIFT OF YOU.

THAT GREAT RAISE...
COMMUNION FLYS ITSELF!
THE GREAT RAYS SING,
GRACE.

Divine Intent expresses Fulfillment
as the very Nature of all Life.

this boundless Earth knows
Our timeless Consciousness.
Meaning Lights Our Mutual
experience of Movement.
song rises as our Individual
and Universal throats Register
the Bright Alignment.
Our Heaven's Gate Is
We the people Being
the Earth gate.

THE CONNECTION YOU EMBRACE
AT THE CENTER OF YOUR BEING UNCOVERS,
THRU YOUR EXPERIENCE OF FEELING,
THE EXQUISITE BEAUTY OF REALITY.

Sovereignty means Being
the Presence of Security
without the exercise of power.
It Is the Ultimate Genuineness.

Yielding to the Unfoldment
of the Movement of Creation
Is You Embodying Your Wholeness
thru Gratitude and Trust.

All of Us Are Soul
Being brothers and sisters
effortlessly Innocent.

CHOOSE FOR YOUR INNER PEACE
AND YOU ENTER THE REALM OF MEANING.

© 1900
F.A. RINEHART
OMAHA

THE LAST SHAMAN ALLOWS FOR
THE RELEASE OF ALL PARAPHERNALIA
(INCLUDING THE NEED FOR TREATIES)
AND SO EXPERIENCES
THE UNITY THAT IS ALWAYS BEING.
WHEN WE CHOOSE TO CONSCIOUSLY
EMBODY THAT UNITY, TO ACCEPT OUR
TOTALITY, TO EMBRACE OUR DIVINITY,
EACH ONE OF US IS
THE LAST SHAMAN.

AS THOUGHTS OF DUALITY AND CONCEPTS
OF POLARITY ARE MINDSETS THAT DEFINE
A WORLD OF LIMITATION - IN WHICH NEGATIVITY
SEEMS TO APPEAR - A PHOTOGRAPHIC NEGATIVE
IS A DARK, STILL PICTURE OF A PICTURE.
BUT NOW, WHEN ALL THAT TRULY IS LIGHT
IS "EXPOSED" TO THE LIGHT. . .

"YOU CAN NOT MOVE A MOUNTAIN
THAT IS NOT ALREADY MOVING."

RAJPUR, 1993

THE LION AND THE EAGLE
HAVE CROSST THE THRESHOLD TOGETHER.
THE ALPHA AND OMEGA...
ATTENTION CONNECTS.

attention connects...